NATIONAL GEOGRAPHIC

In the Garden

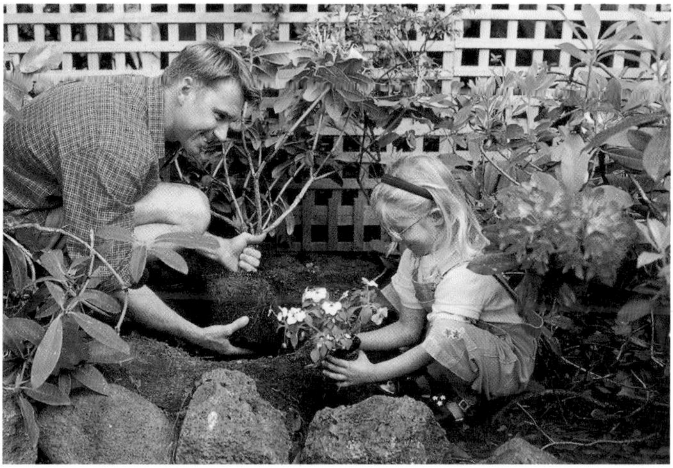

Rose Lorenzo

T0308248

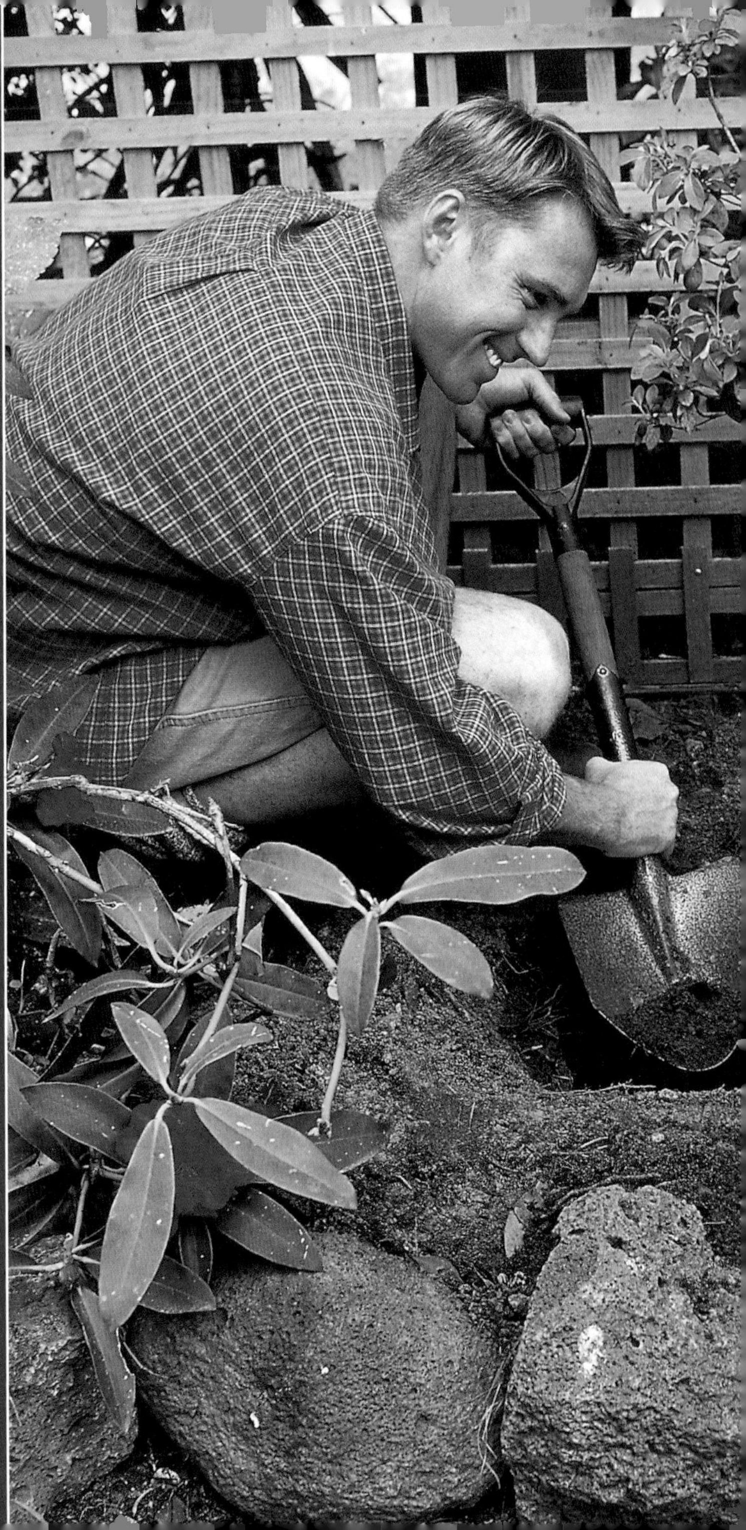

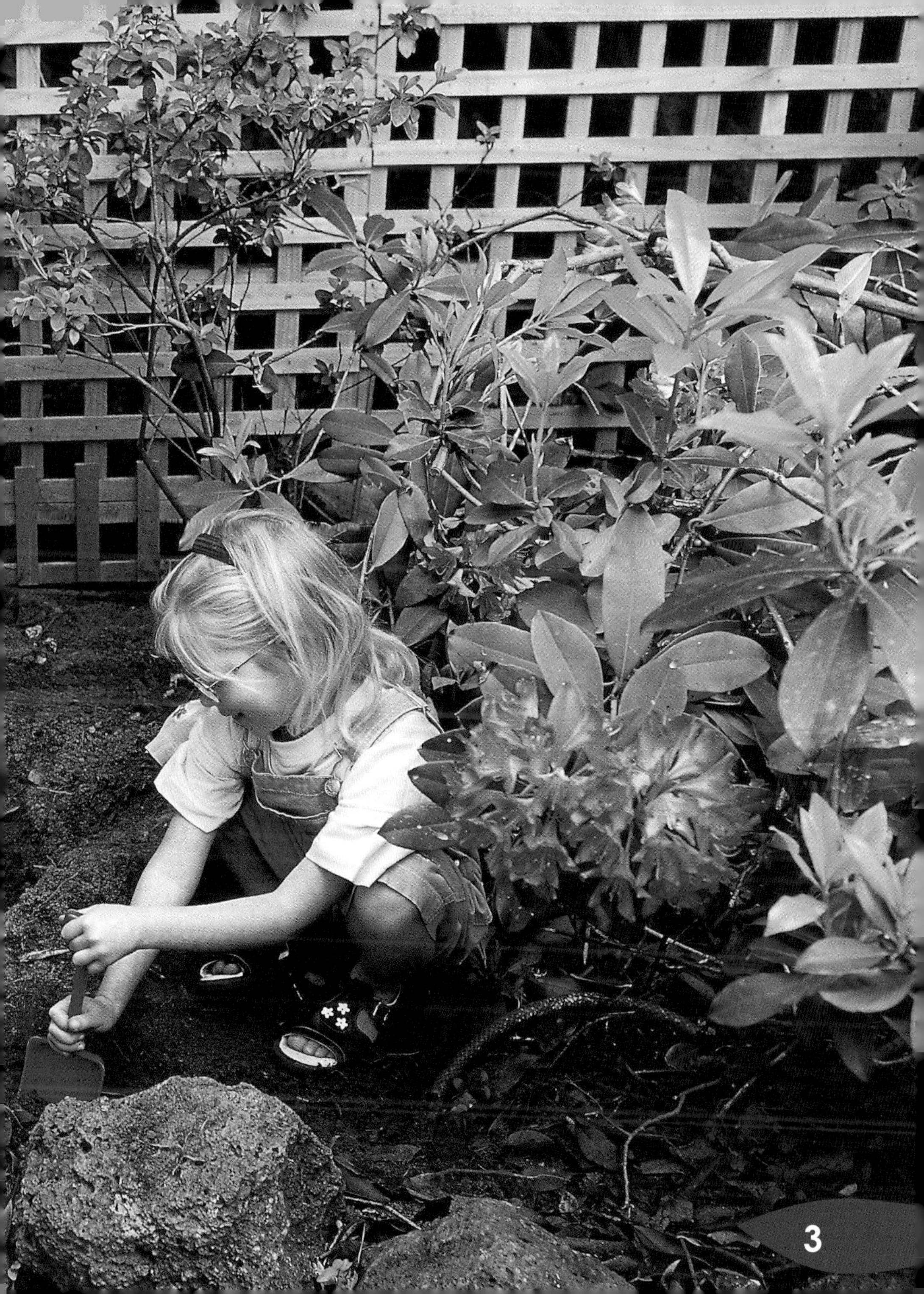

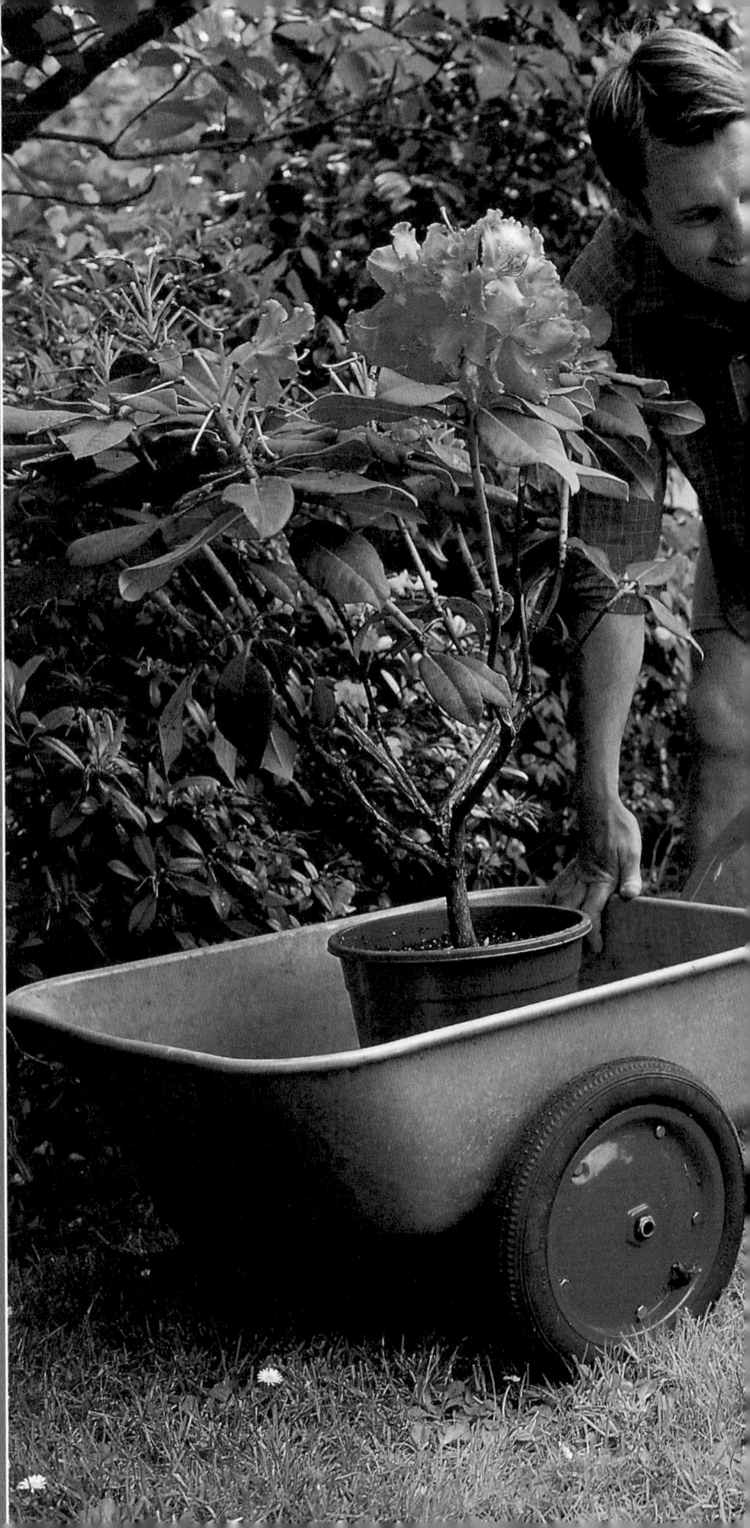

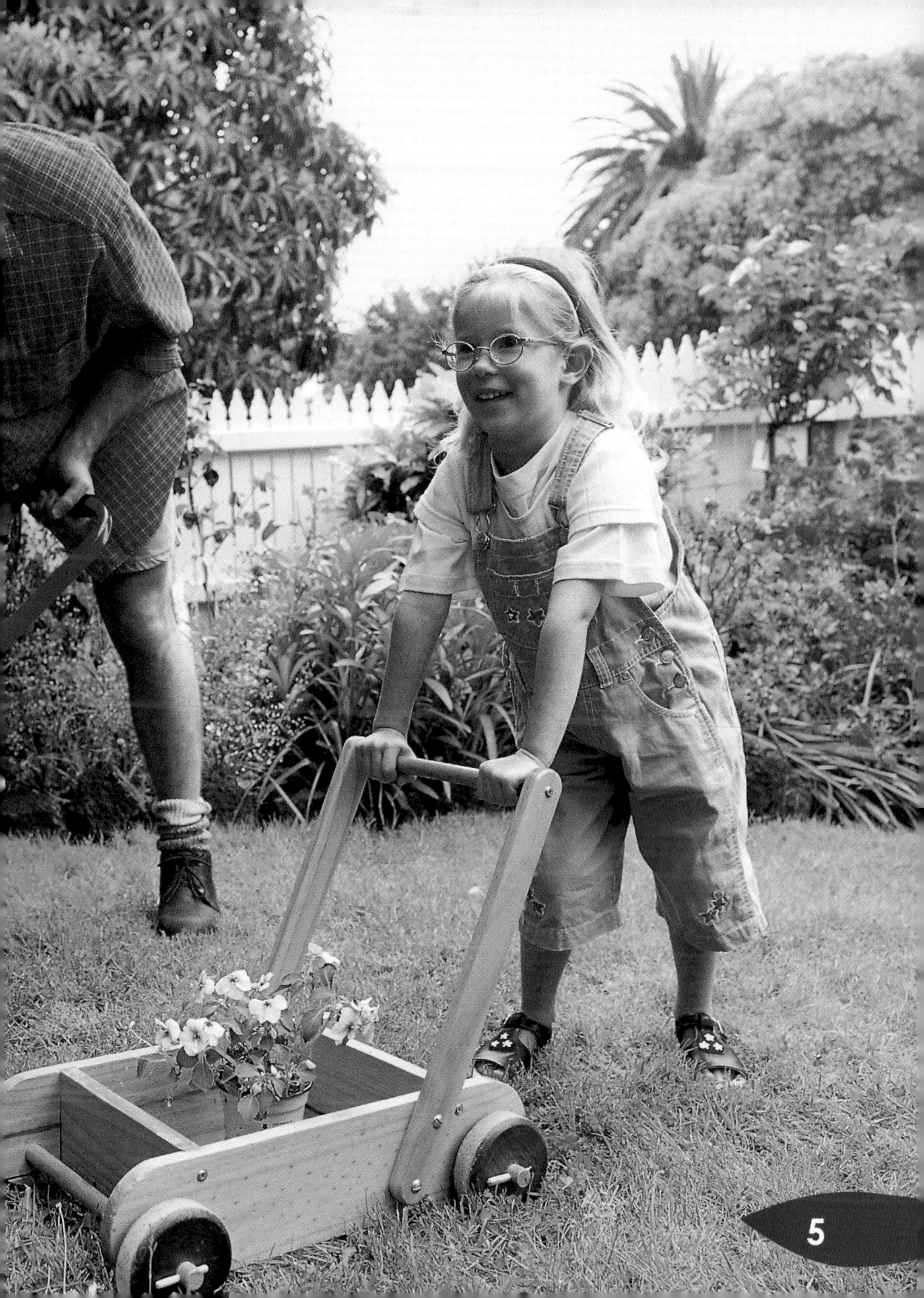

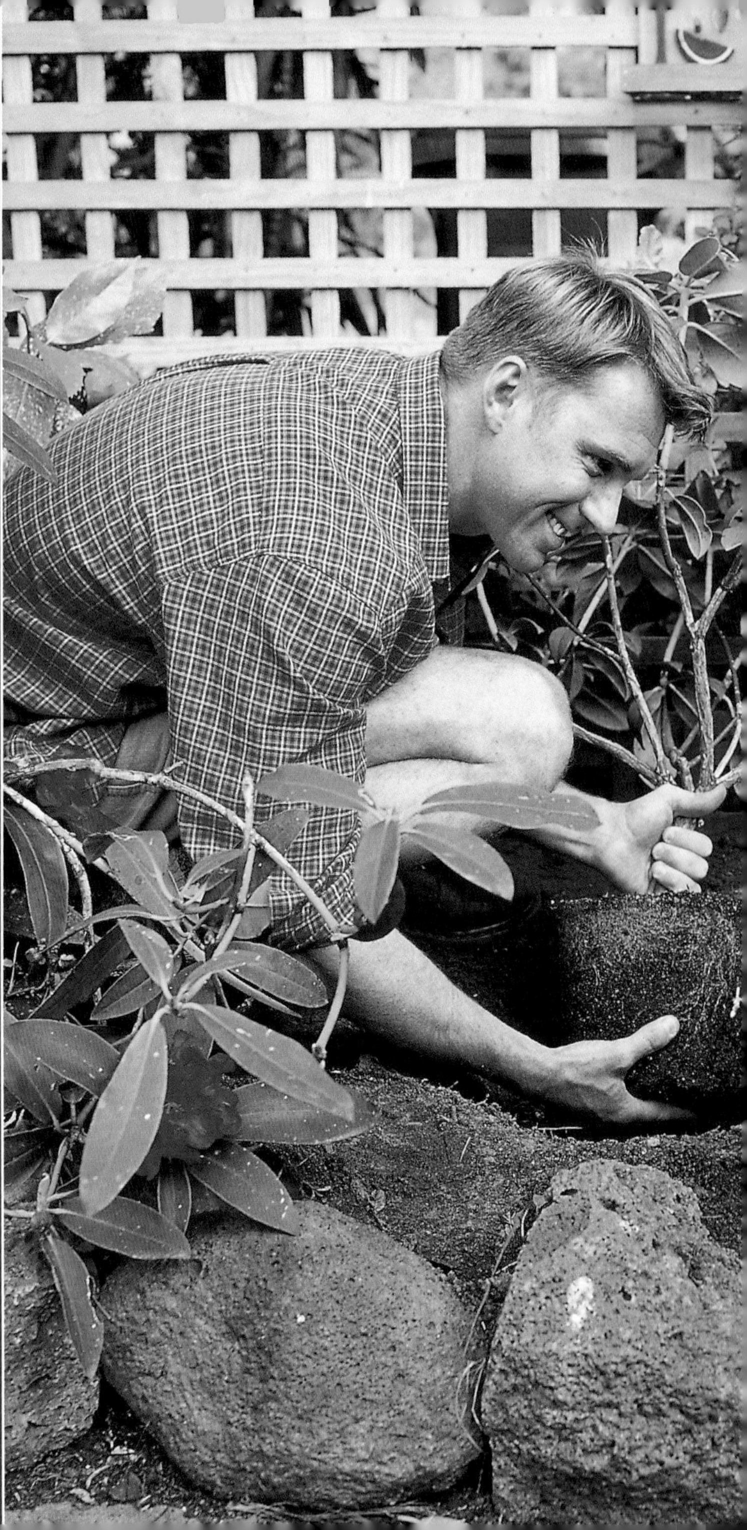

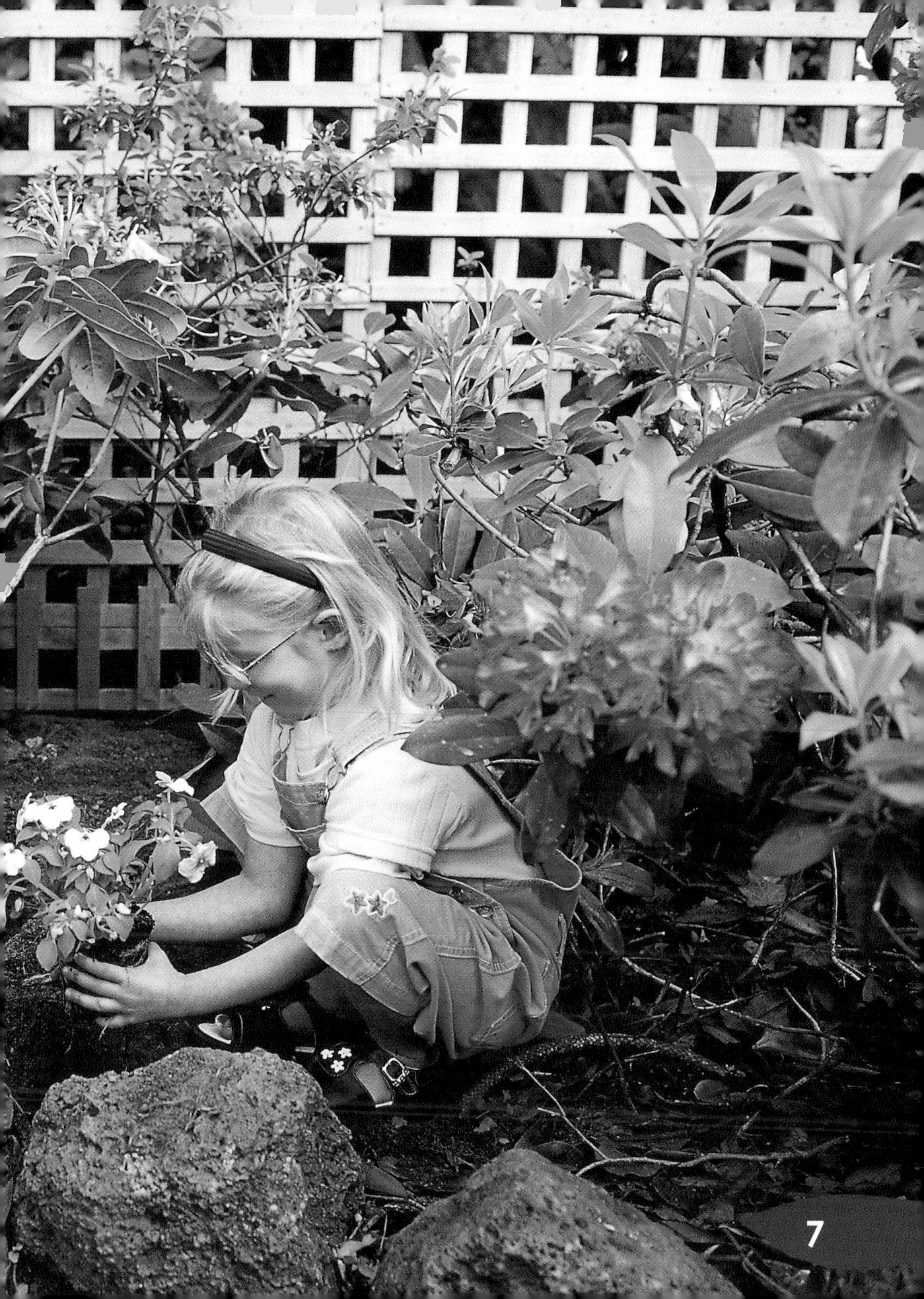

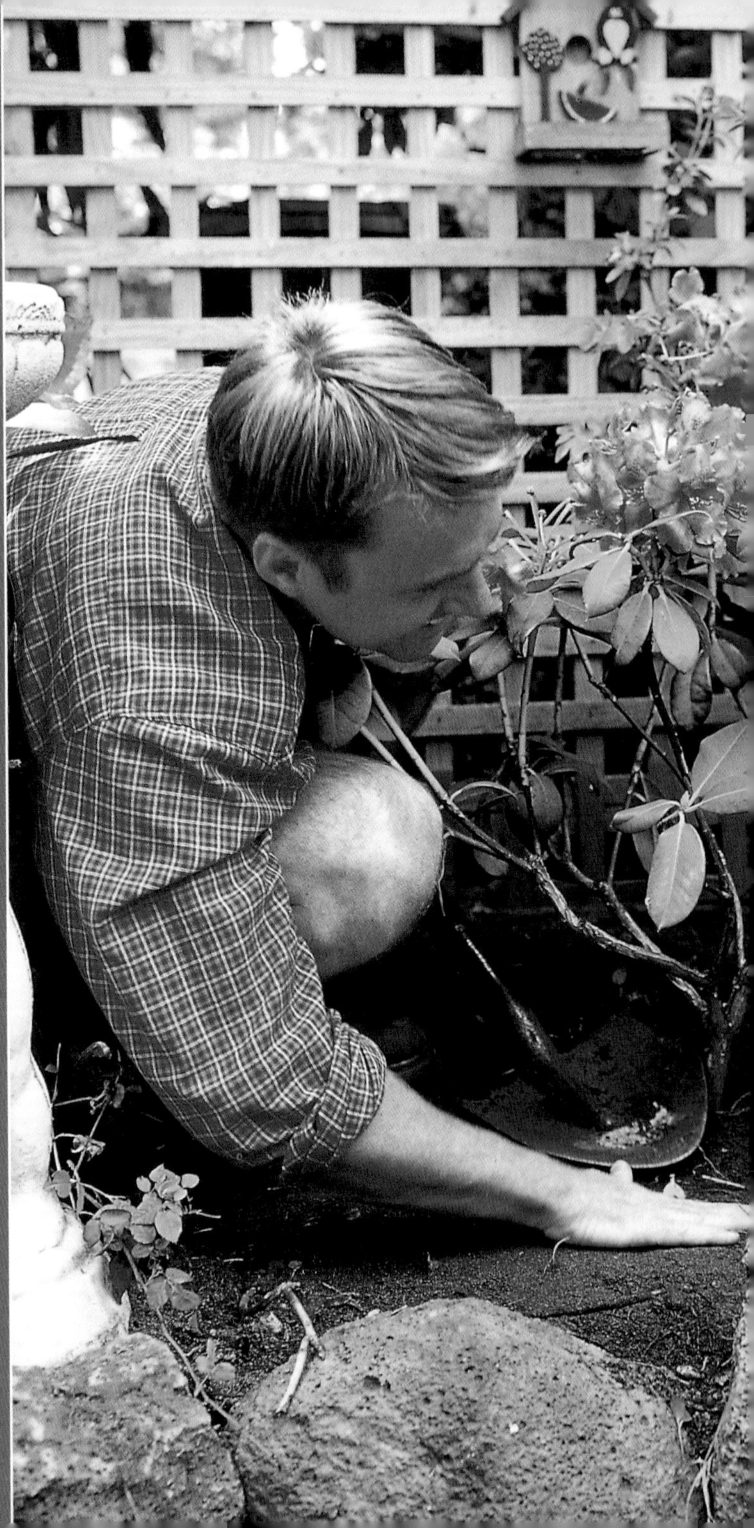

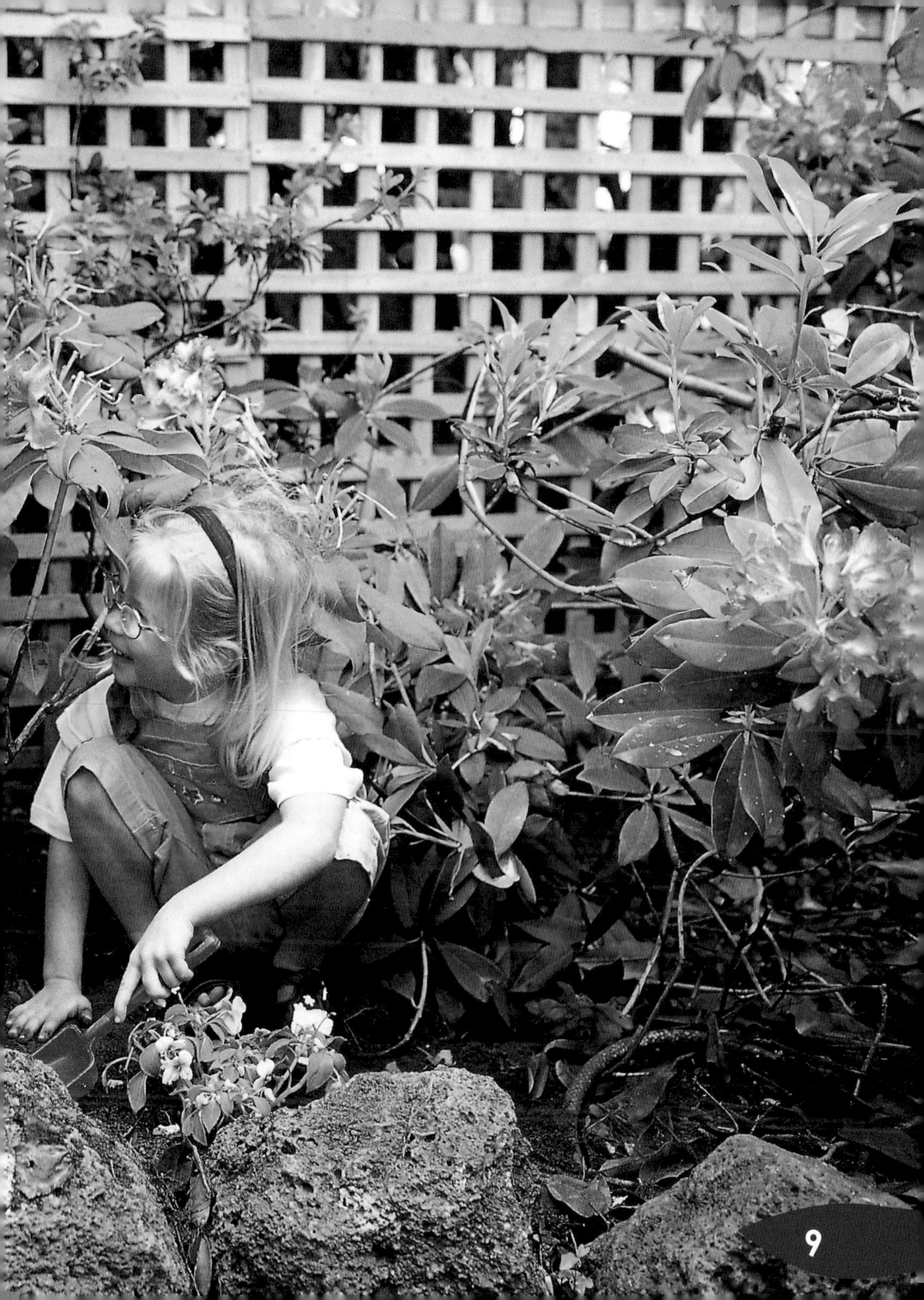

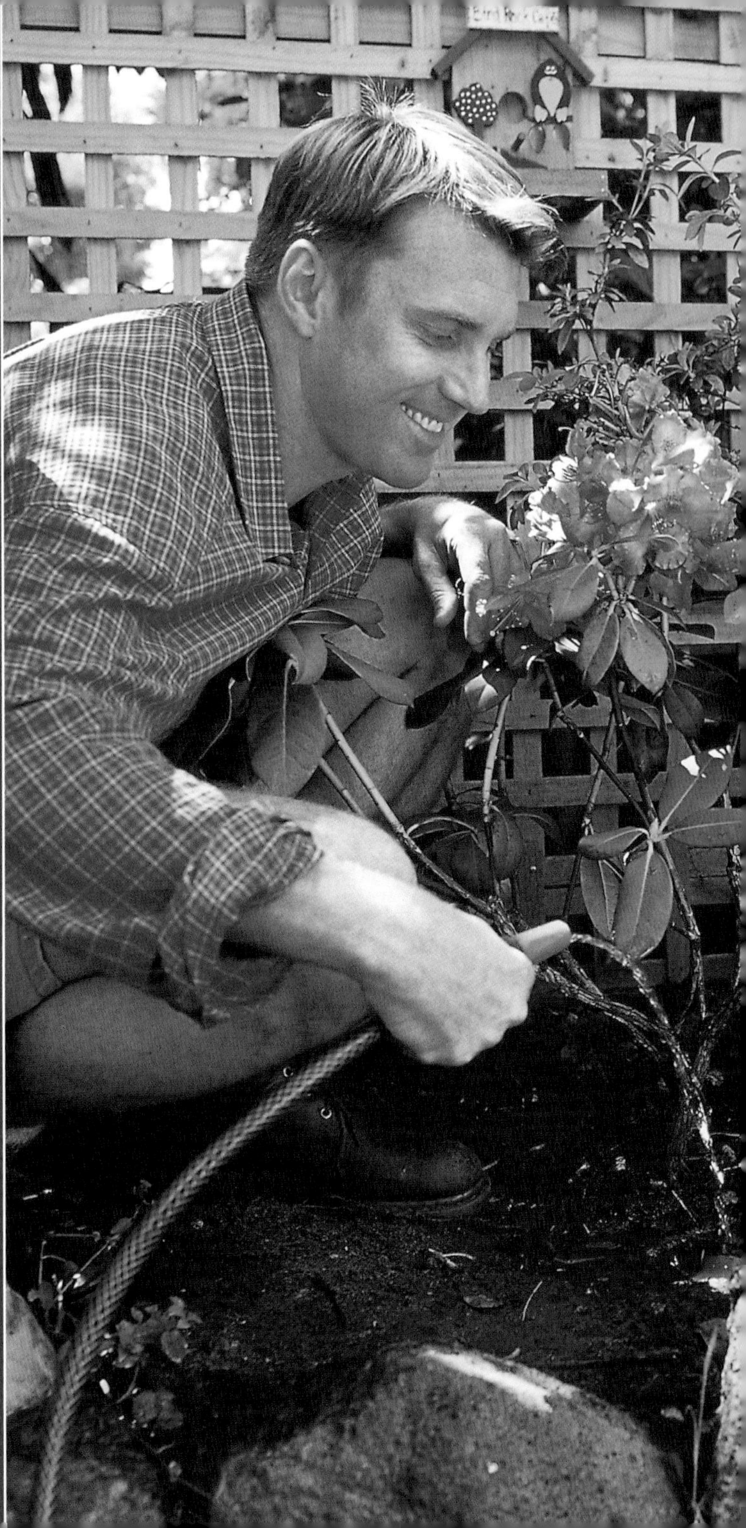

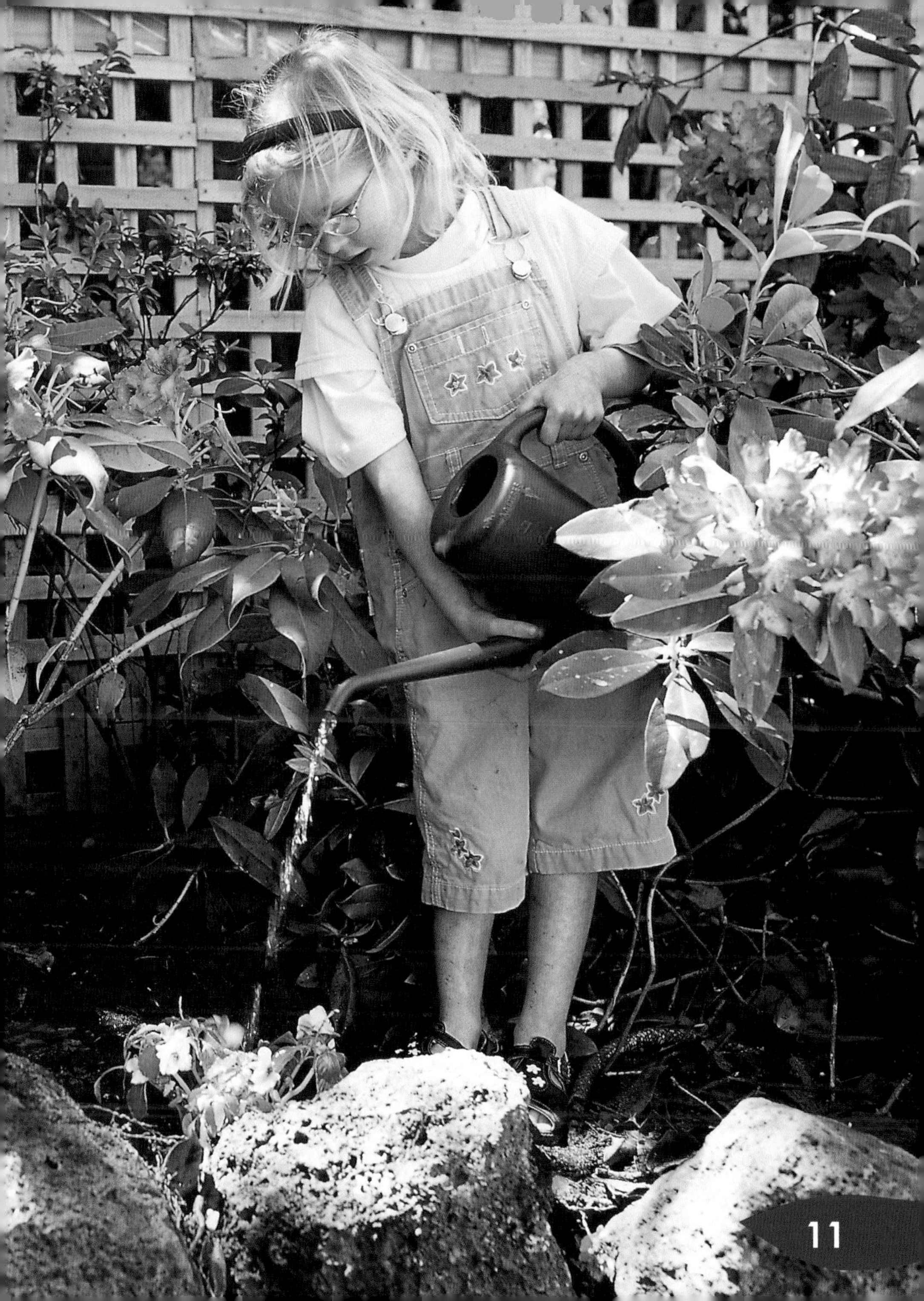

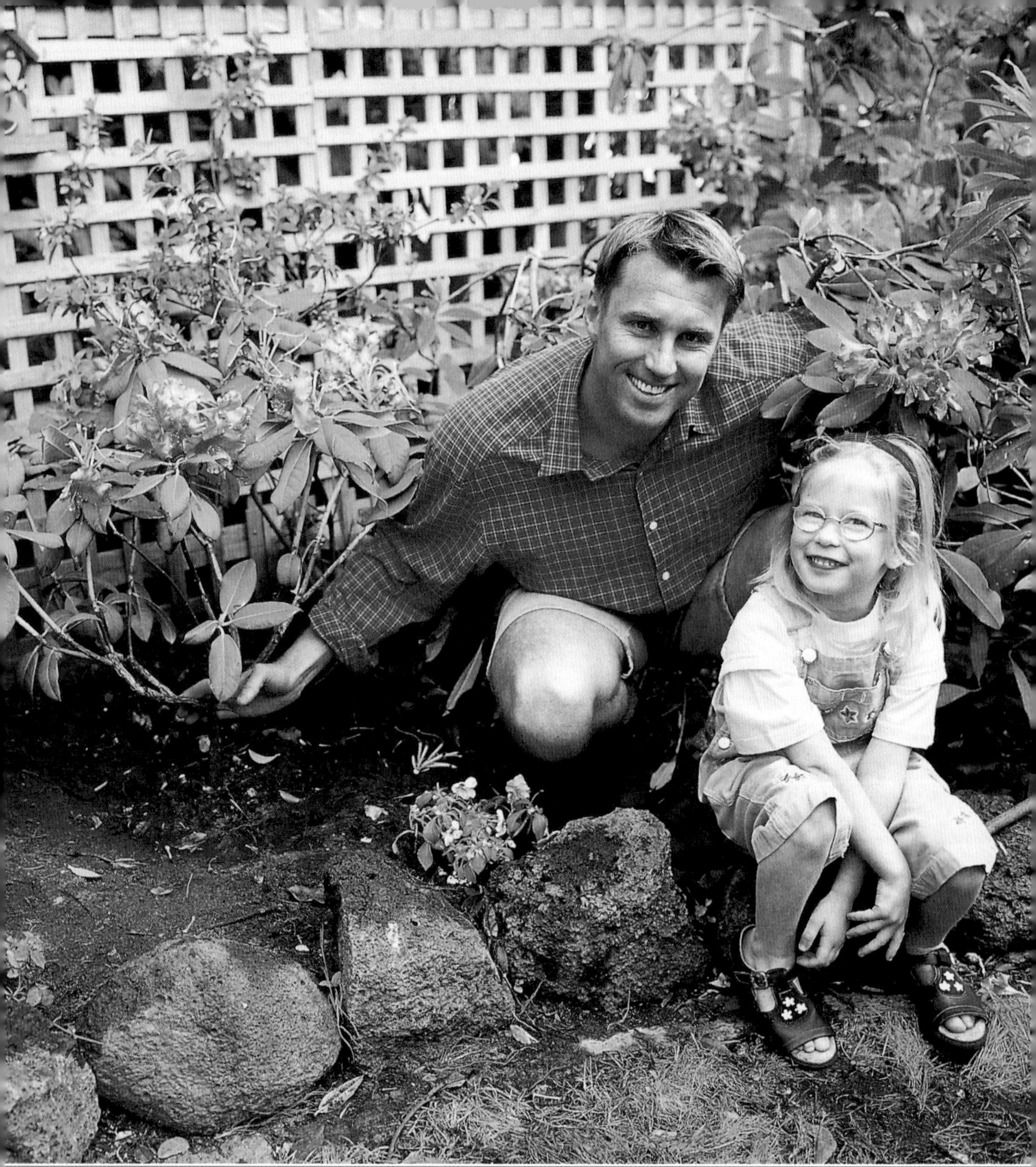